T0171545

Glimpses of Glory

Peggy A. Keady

WestBow
PRESS

A DIVISION OF THOMAS NELSON

ISBN: 978-1-4497-6443-2 (sc)
ISBN: 978-1-4497-6444-9 (hc)
ISBN: 978-1-4497-6442-5 (e)

Library of Congress Control Number: 2012915067

WestBow Press books may be ordered through booksellers or by contacting:

WestBow Press
A Division of Thomas Nelson
1663 Liberty Drive
Bloomington, IN 47403
www.westbowpress.com
1-(866) 928-1240

Printed in the United States of America

WestBow Press rev. date: 09/28/2012

For my family and friends.

Families are not always made by birth or dwelling,
but by shared smiles, hugs, and dreams.
—Unknown

He [God] has kept this secret for centuries and generations past, but now at last it has pleased him to tell it to those who love him and live for him, and the riches and glory of his plan are for you Gentiles, too. And this is the secret: *that Christ in your hearts is your only hope of glory.*

Colossians 1:26–27 LB

Table of Contents

The Invitation

Foreword

We are all familiar with the saying that, while it's impossible for us to choose our family, we can indeed choose our friends. When Peggy Keady relocated to my hometown of Kosciusko, Mississippi, she chose me as her family physician. Since that day, our physician-patient relationship has evolved into a special friendship as multifaceted as a priceless diamond.

My family and I have come to anticipate Peggy's lovingly crafted Christmas letters as much as any beautifully wrapped holiday gift. Her thought-provoking "A View from the Pew" newsletter articles reflect insights, feelings, and truths that reveal the genuine depth of this author's Christian faith. Although entitled *Glimpses of Glory*, this compilation of her "Christmas Letters" and "Faith Notes" provides an unobstructed view of Peggy's love for her fellow man and for her Savior. It is indeed an honor to call her "friend."

Stanley Hartness, MD

Preface

Sixteen years ago, I decided to write an annual Christmas letter and send it as I would a Christmas card to my family and friends. In it I would share my thoughts, my feelings, and my insights about life and the Christian faith.

The response from friends was overwhelmingly positive. They are the ones who have continually urged me over the years to consider publishing my work.

My other writings arose from serving as the director of pastoral visitation for several years at my church, First United Methodist Church, Kosciusko, Mississippi. While functioning as director, I began writing an article each month for the church newsletter first under the byline, "A Pastoral Note," and then under the byline, "A View from the Pew." Though I am no longer on staff, I was given the opportunity to continue my article writing, which I greatly enjoy. Since these writings also have brought and continue to bring a similar positive response, I have chosen to include them under the title "Faith Notes."

Peggy A. Keady

Acknowledgments

I am grateful to the following individuals for their informed guidance and skillful assistance in helping with the preparation of my writings for submission to WestBow Press:

Judge William C. Keady, my father, who inspired me by writing his autobiography, *All Rise*, and having it published shortly before his death. His book is a priceless treasure of mine.

Hugh B. McCormick III for his knowledge and wisdom regarding book marketing and publishing.

Brandt Nichols for his willingness to share important information about computer publishing.

Diane Boutwell Grey for typing the manuscript and providing grammatical guidance.

Carolyn Pilgrim for making herself available for numerous consultations about the world of books.

William C. Keady Jr. for his wisdom and commonsense suggestions during the preparation of the manuscript.

Stanley Hartness, MD, for graciously consenting to write the foreword for *Glimpses of Glory.*

Christy Curry of Curry Photography, for her generosity in providing the author's photograph for the back cover.

Teresa Toten for her technical advice and assistance.

Trisha Oakes for her help with the computer in saving the final edit.

Vicki Parker for aiding in the execution of numerous required computer tasks.

Charlsie Russell, author and owner, Loblolly Writer's House, for her excitement about writing and her willingness to comment on my work.

The combined expertise and knowledge of these talented individuals has been invaluable in refining my writings.

Christmas Letters

My Heart's Litany

Come, precious friends; give thanks with me to God, our Creator and Savior for:

The beauty of autumn leaves, Christmas trees, and lacy spiderwebs
  tinged with dew,
The smells of newly mowed grass, burning leaves, coffee roasting,
  gardenias, fir trees, and cottonseed oil,
The white of cotton in the fields and the glitter of fresh-fallen snow;
The mists rising off ponds on a frosty morn,
The glow of beautiful sunsets and the glimmers of first light at dawn,
The blue skies that follow the storm clouds,
The sounds of whip-poor-wills calling in the night and geese honking
  to their comrades in flight,
The pealing of church bells and the wailing of bagpipes,
The mighty swell of the pipe organ and the mellow tone of a saxophone,
The sobbing in the night and the laughter in the light,
The voices of those we love and hymns about the Lord above,
The whisper of the wind in the leaves, and the songs of cicadas in
  the trees,
The splash of raindrops, the rush of roaring streams, and the cadence
  of waves upon the shore.
All these wonders bid us come and Thee adore.

The feel of summer warmth and winter chill, clean sheets on beds,
  and crisp dollar bills,
The cool of silk and the heat of wool, the texture of fuzzy coats and
  silky curls,
The velvet touch of a horse's coat and the relief a lemon gives a
  scratchy throat,
The smile of a child, the wrinkles of a gran, and the posture of a soldier,
The strength of a man,

The taste of homemade ice cream, cookies, and jam, and theater
    popcorn,
Cinnamon and ham, greens and cornbread, nuts and cake, fried
    catfish, and chocolate milkshakes,
The ideas of freedom and justice for all, peace on earth, forgiveness,
    and grace,
The truth that God loves us,
The news that Jesus saves,
The time to be loving,
The reason: He gave.

Through the days of our lives
So many yet few,
I give grateful thanks for the hours spent with you.

1996

My Prayer

When I behold
The morning sun of pink and gold,
I stand in awe
With gaping jaw
And count each wonder that unfolds.

The shine of dew upon the ground,
The silent early morning sound,
The wakening cry of early birds,
The lowing call of cattle herds.

A leaf, a stone, a fragrant smell,
The marvels of our world they tell.
I touch the earth on bended knee
And say a prayer for you and me.

Dear God, be near to us, I pray.
Thank You for giving us another day.
May we look up and see Your face
In every person and in every place.

1997

Peace Meal

What, dear friends, should I write
On this cold and wintry night,
To lift your soul and cheer your heart,
To let you know we're set apart
For glorious things?

The skies of pink and gold and blue
God made especially for me and you.
The trees and shrubs that give us air:
The Creator's love placed them there.

The many creatures, both tame and wild,
Were fashioned so to bring a smile
Upon our faces when life is tough,
And we're prone to say we've had enough.

The light of hope a candle brings
In the darkest night when angels sing
Is just a hint of God's great plan
To redeem the world by becoming man.

This brings to mind a message sweet
About a baby born and nearby sheep,
The stable crude, the parents two,
The wise men three, and me and you.

Have you listened to the Christmas tunes
Of peace on earth, Jesus is coming soon?
Through frosty air and Christmas lights
The stars proclaim, "O Holy Night."

God's peace to you this night, dear friend,
Wherever you may dwell.
For Christ, our Lord, the reigning King,
Declares that "all is well!"

1998

Heart Light

Dear God of glory and marvelous light,
What can I send my friends this night?

I know You are nearer than hands and feet.
So now as I enter my retreat
I ask of You, dear Savior bright,
To bless my friends and ease their plight.

So clear and glistening are the beams
That round about Your presence gleam,
I bow my head and kneel to start
A psalm of praise from a joyful heart.

If only I could see Your light,
I would never fail in living right
Amid the gloom of earthly cares.
I know Your healing light repairs.

During the storm that often rages,
I know Your light shines through the ages.
The star that shepherds saw so long ago
I see it still with its dazzling glow.

To You who said, "I am the Light,"
I yield my heart this Christmas night.

1999

The Spirit of Christmas Past

I stand at the grave of my mom and sigh,
"Was it only in June that we said good-bye?"
To me it seems like a hundred years
Since her dear, sweet voice graced my ears;
How I long to see her precious face
And hold her small frame in my embrace.
Yet that is part of Christmas past
Not made by God to forever last.

I remember the years when we were young
And stockings by the chimney were hung.
They were full of surprises and tasty treats
Far more than Bill and I could ever eat!
The music carried out over the air,
As carols were heard everywhere.
We were told the baby Jesus was coming
And that Santa Claus was in flight.
I treasure these memories;
I recall them with delight.
Yet they are part of Christmas past
Not made by God to forever last.

I stand at the grave of my mom and pray,
Thanking the Lord for her life and His way.
Mom lived in a manner that brought honor to all.
Thinking about her leaves me enthralled.
I ask God to show me His will in some way.
Just what's to be done by night and by day?
"Fear not, Peg and Bill," He whispers from on high,
"Your mom is with me, and she will never die.
Carry on with your lives and always know
Her presence is with you wherever you go."

I take a deep breath as I walk to my car
For I'm following, you see, that same natal star.
It's been part of our family for Christmases past
And was made by God to forever last.

As you stand in your home on this holy night,
Reach out to your loved ones and hug them tight.
Celebrate the memories of Christmas past
And to the natal star, always hold fast.

2000
Dedicated to the glory of God and in loving memory of my mother,
Dorothy Thompson Keady (1913–2000).

Christmas Prayer

Recently on a winter's night
As I lay resting without fright,
I sensed a light from up above
Bidding me rise and see God's love.

I stood transfixed and watched in awe
As angels in my room I saw.
Their faces shone with dazzling flames
As each gave glory to His name.
The Christ, the Holy One of God
Who gave His life for men of sod.

The angels sang in glorious voice
The wonders of His rugged cross
And told me while I barely breathed
Of plans He has for you and me.

He desires our lives, not some, but all
And pours on us His holy call.
While babies sleep and angels sing,
We've been called to serve the King.

How awesome is the gift we hold.
It's far more valuable than gold.
With bated breath we kneel and pray
And rejoice in Christ, our Lord, the Way.

2001
Dedicated to the glory of God and to the precious memories of past Christmases
with family and friends who now behold our Savior face-to-face.

Love's Winter Song

O God of grace and glory,
O King of love and might,
I love to tell your story
Morning, noon, and night.

I've been to the edge of this life
And watched one I love enter in,
To the mystery of heaven and no strife,
To the wonderful absence of sin.

My heart is broken yet joyful,
A paradoxical mixture, 'tis true,
For love cannot resist the pull
Of resurrection when this life is through.

I see the glow of Your beauty,
The trees reaching up in a plea.
I feel the light of Your presence
Continually abiding with me.

"Walk on, walk on," You say,
"For your journey is not yet done.
I've chosen you, I'll take your hand
Until life's course is run."

"Look up, dear one, with tear-filled eyes.
Behold your Lord and King.
Your life, like hers, is held in trust
Till I shall come again."

"And on that day your face will shine
As all around you there will be
Your loved ones gathered at the gate
When I call you home to be with Me."

All I have to say is "Glory, glory, glory!"
Death is just a door in the resurrection story.
She is not dead, she does not sleep.
I feel such joy, I cannot weep.

She suffered long and trod her road;
Her pain is over, she's lost her load.
What peace I feel to know she's free.
If I cry now, it's just for me.

I was with her when she breathed her last;
She squeezed my hand, and then she passed.
I cradled her body and hugged her tight
As I said good-bye to my friend of light.

I know she sees Christmas with Easter eyes
As she looks at life from heaven's side.
Often I pray to let God know
My thanks to Him that He loves us so.

To you, my friends, I send this prayer
With love and thanks for all we share.
Give praise to our God this Christmastide
For He promises always with us to abide.

2002

Dedicated to the glory of God and in loving memory
of Diamond Boardman Brown(1922–2002).

On the Road to Christmas

On the road to Christmas,
What wonders I have seen!
The blue and pink of winter skies
With gold streaks in between.

The deer that bound across the road
Alert with eagle eyes
And vanish in the tall, thick woods
That run on either side.

The cougar that dashes cross the bank
At the Big Black River's edge
His agile body, sleek and trim,
As he clears a sandy ledge.

The cows and horses in the fields
With calves and foals nearby
Spend their days, content to graze,
In grasses low and high.

The raindrops falling all around
As the trees sway to and fro
While cool winds blow the last leaves down
And streams fill up and overflow.

All things point to God above
Who gave His Son to bear our sin
And fashioned us to live in love,
So Jesus died and rose again.

He lives today along the road
And longs to spend some time with you.
He knows the way to lift your load
But only if you want Him to.

The choice is yours, it's plain to see,
You can choose to travel the road alone
Or decide you prefer His company
And in so doing find your true home.

As you travel the Road to Christmas,
May your trip be good and your troubles few,
And in this brand New Year,
May God bless you.

2003
Dedicated to the glory of God and in memory and honor of traveling companions
I have spent time with through the years on the road to Christmas.

Glory Revealed

These days it's Mi-Ling, W. C. Monk, and me:
She's almost fifteen, he's ageless, and I'm sixty-three.
We pass our days in a virtual whirl
'Cause it's early to rise for this working girl!

I travel before seven, thirty miles to my post,
Enjoy all the children and roll home in "coast."
Highway 14 takes me over hill and dale
By grazing livestock and hay in round bales.

I often see deer on the road I ride down.
They stand quiet and erect, listening to sounds.
Whatever they hear may cause them to flee.
They'll either cross over or disappear in the trees.

The music plays softly as I view a golden sky.
I hear "The Glory of the Lord" amplified.
I take a deep breath as my eyes overflow.
What wonder! What grandeur! The Lord does bestow.

Do you see it? Do you hear it, dear friend of my heart?
Come right now; ride with me; soon we'll depart,
To see skies filled with never-ending hues
Of pinks, grays, golds, lavenders, and blues.

We'll catch a glimpse of clouds scurrying by
Peppered with birds as they rise up to fly.
Whether rainy, sunny, or snowy, they roam
With an inborn compass that leads them all home.

We'll pull our jackets snug when day turns to night
And watch as the stars twinkle into sight.
The cool, crisp wind blowing through our hair
Opens up our minds and makes us aware.

We'll pause as we recall the Babe in the stable:
The Savior, the Christ, the God who is able.
This Christmas we bow in humility and awe,
Rejoicing in Jesus who fulfilled all the law.

"Give hope," He whispers, "as the needy reach out.
Walk in faith with My power. It works; never doubt.
Be at peace with your brother; My love will mend.
Remember that I love you and My love never ends."

2004
Dedicated to the glory of God and in
loving honor of my brother, William Colbert Keady Jr.

Christmas Reflections

Gazing through the cottage window at the lake below,
The colors reflected from the sky above give a heavenly glow
The changing shades of gold and blue and pink and grey.
All signal the end to another passing day.

The trees remain covered in their autumn gowns
Until the wind whips by and tears them down.
Their leaves twist and turn in graceful falls;
Then land in piles along the walls.

The birds overhead are winging south in flight
To reach warmer climes by tomorrow's winter night.
The song they sing to those above
Tells of humans below, seeking the God of love.

This beautiful old story is both simple and fine.
It's about God's great plan to deliver mankind
By sending His Son as a little sweet child
To be born, to live, and to preach awhile.

God the Father gave his only Son, our lives to win,
Then blessed Jesus with strength to overcome sin.
So the Savior died, giving His life for all
And rose from the tomb, canceling Adam's fall.

This world we share is in great distress
As governments decide to allow Him less.
It's time for us to boldly declare
That Jesus is Lord and show that we care.

The Good News of Christmas is our gift, you see,
For we can help the world from evil to flee,
And find in Christ Jesus, the King of Kings,
The peace we seek, which only He can bring.

Tonight as you prepare to take your rest
Fall on your knees and offer your best,
Pray to the Father, who is listening above,
Having sent His Son in sacrificial love.

Ask that His power be poured on those near
So this Christmas Season many may hear
And experience the Savior, who came as a child
And grew to manhood and walked the last mile.

Rejoice! O rejoice! Precious friends of my heart,
For Jesus, our Savior will never depart.
We have peace, His peace which removes all fear,
So let us go courageously into this, His New Year!

2005
Dedicated to the glory of God and in honor of my nephew, Jeffrey Wayne Keady,
his wife, Susan Nelson Keady, and their son, Aaron Ruston Keady.

Snow Hope

The trees are bare as I stand and stare,
And the sky is a steely gray,
While the pundits preach, "There is no hope."
In that old familiar way.

Yet in my heart I hear a song.
It never stops, so I sing along,
"He was born, He died, He rose, He lives!
Rejoice! Rejoice! New life He gives."

The truth rings out across the seas
There is a God who hears our pleas,
The snow falls softly on the ground
As angel throngs make heavenly sounds.

The Word has come for all to hear
Good News! There's hope, for Christ is here!
Put doubt, despair, and worry to flight
For God has sent redemption's light.

Hope lies hidden beneath the snow
Where rushing, living waters flow.
Just reach down and brush the flakes
And see the forms that new life takes.

2006
Dedicated to the glory of God and in loving memory of
Mary Ann Kemp (1934–2006), whose friendship and example of love
greatly warmed my life and the lives of countless others.

Winter's Embers

On one cold, wet, and dreary day,
I chanced to see a flaming tree.
The bright red leaves it displayed
Blazed like fire for all to see.

It dazzled as it shivered in the wind
With leaves aglow on every side.
Then as the branches bent down low
The leaves fell off and died.

This made me wonder as I watched
How faith within grows bright,
And then as we age it ripens,
Then takes on God's full light.

My own prayer is to age with grace,
To one day reach a flaming end,
To be filled with God's glorious light
And be blessed with His amen.

As autumn's fire burns down to winter's embers,
I pray for you, dear friends of old,
May the love we share be long remembered
And the warm light of Christ stir your precious soul.

2007
Dedicated to the glory of God and in loving honor of Joseph and Martha Mims
(1932–2011).

Encounter in the Woods

Into the autumnal woods I ran,
Seeking for God with outstretched hands.
I knew He would meet me if I went
In an attitude of prayer with both knees bent.

In a patch of sun at the tree trunk's root,
He breathed a word that struck me mute.
His whispers came as bolts of might
And filled my heart with radiant light.

He told of some who have gone astray
Who no longer walk in His holy way.
Yet we who love Him can turn the tide
If in prayer and His love we still abide.

The holy Christ child came into view,
The Savior and Lord of me and you.
He asked me to call you, His child, to pray
For all people everywhere this Christmas Day.

Let us do as He bids, with our hands lifted high.
Let us praise and adore, Him alone magnify,
For His image we bear and we're called by His name.
May all glory be His, with each life He reclaims.

2008

Dedicated to the glory of God and in loving honor of my dear friend Jim Mancke.

Holy Silence

The trees are bare;
The leaves are down;
My heart is emptied out;
There's silence all around.

I wait in barren stillness
For the sounds of those I love,
But all I hear is my beating heart,
Then a fluttering from above.

As I close my eyes and kneel to pray,
My ears are keenly honed
When the Spirit whispers at my back,
"Dear one, you're not alone."

"With healing in His wings,
The Lord has come today
To do in you His saving work
And wash your pain away."

The Lord comes in and lights the room
As memories fill my mind
Of days gone by with kith and kin
And Jesus at my side.

His nearness soothes my aching heart
And fills the empty space
With peace and love and gentleness,
Trademarks of His embrace.

His first Advent did change my life
For "born again" I am.
His ministry this day to me
Says I am His precious lamb.

I rise to meet the hallowed dawn
With God who leads me on
To greater love and deeds of light
For the glory of His Son.

2009

Dedicated to the glory of God and in loving honor of my friend of many years,
Julia Blackburn Crittenden (1935–2011), whom I affectionately call JuJu.

In the Midst

In the midst of joy—there's sorrow;
Out of today will come tomorrow.

Where there's dark—there's also Light
As we recall that holy night.

In the midst of sin—the Savior came
To cleanse and make us whole again.

In the midst of pain—there comes a peace;
His gentle voice makes hurting cease.

In the midst of want—our needs are met
By caring ones who charge no debt.

In the midst of loss—comfort abounds
As we meet the Lord on holy ground.

In the midst of Christmas—
Wondrous things I see.

Like angels, shepherds, and the wise men three;
Mary and Joseph and the Messiah Baby.

The bright star in the night—with songs sung above,
All heralding the news of the Gospel of Love.

Draw near, dear ones, and bask in the Light
Of the One in your midst every day and each night.

We are the reason He came to redeem;
He now lives in our midst His power to stream.

Rejoice and be glad—our Savior is near
Forever and always to banish our fear.

2010
Dedicated to the glory of God and in loving honor of my friend of many years,
Dr. Sandra Gail Kennedy, senior pastor of Whole Life Ministries, Augusta, Georgia.

Everlasting Past

Window panes laced with frost
Remind me of the ones I've lost.
Their faces pass before my eyes
As precious memories fall and rise.

How good were those sweet yesterdays
With carols, feasts, and Christmas plays.
We shared the thrill of Jesus' birth,
That holy night He came to earth.

Our hearts were filled with awesome joy
As we beheld God's baby boy.
His hands were lifted toward the sky
Where angels sang a lullaby.

The earth was blessed the day He came;
There's salvation only in His name.
Our days fly by at record speed
As we live out what He decreed.

The dearest gifts in life are friends
With whom we share our outs and ins.
My prayer for you this Christmastide:
"May His love and peace with you abide."

2011
Dedicated to the glory of God and in loving honor of
my beloved friend of many years, Meg Way.

Faith Notes

A Trip to Remember

Commit to the Lord whatever you do, and your plans
will succeed. (Proverbs 16:3 NIV)

That's what we did, Diane Grey and I, before we embarked on the
trip of a lifetime. It was the right way to start, and what a trip we
had! From Kosciusko to Oxford, Mississippi and then to Memphis
flying Delta to New York, where we boarded the ship *Carnival Glory*
for the ports of Saint John, New Brunswick, Canada, and Halifax,
Novia Scotia, Canada.

It'd been a long time since I'd flown (1995) or cruised (1985),
and many things have changed, such as airport security, baggage
allowances and costs, increases in the number of individuals traveling,
the high-tech ways one has to set up a trip, and most of all, I've
changed. I'm older, heavier, less energetic, more easily satisfied with
fewer activities, and no longer enamored by worldly hoopla and
hype. Even though I had spent two years (1964–1966) at New York
Theological Seminary in Manhattan, it seemed as if I was seeing New
York for the first time because it's even more populated now and
completely taken over by the age of computer technology.

Our hotel was located in the middle of Times Square. Even in the
hours past midnight, the sidewalks were filled with masses of people
strolling by shops and vendors enjoying the nightlife of the city. To
me, it was both an amazing and a sobering sight. Each one of those
individuals I saw is someone for whom Jesus Christ died whether that
individual knows it or not.

The beautiful ship *Carnival Glory* was so huge—thirteen decks—
that we were dwarfed as we boarded; but once at sea, it became
like a small cork bobbing up and down. How vast is God's creation!
Meeting twelve of the cast members from the soap opera *The
Guiding Light*, was a special experience for me, as many fun summers
had been spent watching that show with my mom. All the actors and

actresses were very gracious and personable. I will always treasure being a part of that celebrity event—something I could have only imagined years before.

The night in New York attending the musical *South Pacific* and hearing that wonderful music, the delicious meals on the ship, the shore excursions in Canada's cooler temperatures, the gentle seas, the comfortable cabin, the company of a dear friend, and a good book to read—what could be as nice? Only one thing: getting home!

We had a grand trip and made it through all the hassles at airports, at ports, and aboard ship and did what we went to do. Home, however, never looked so good! Thank you, Lord, for watching over us and bringing us safely back to our dwelling place, Kosciusko, Mississippi.

Answered Prayer

The second week of July, I planned to make another trip to Whole Life Ministry in Augusta, Georgia, to see my friend Dr. Sandra Kennedy. I made the motel reservations but then found out the very next day that my traveling companion was unable to go. Naturally, I was disappointed, as I had been excited about having my friend see the Whole Life Church and hear and meet Sandra Kennedy. So I went to plan B: going with my brother to Thomaston, Georgia, to take his grandson back home after a visit to Oxford, Mississippi. I signed back on with them.

Because of God's timing of the events in my life, I was able to go by myself to Sandra's church. I attended a most revealing Bible study on Thursday night, visited with Sandra's secretary and the church's worship leader on Friday morning, and shopped in their excellent bookstore before sitting in on one of the classes on healing ,skillfully taught by the director of the Healing Center. I was treated to lunch at their Honey from the Rock Café and later returned to the hotel, as their guest, to rest until the 7:00 p.m. Healing Explosion service.

I was overwhelmed by their great kindness and generosity to me from my first contact with Sandra's secretary all the way through to my wonderful one-on-one visit with Sandra after the Healing Explosion service. She and I had a wonderful time at the restaurant talking and laughing. It was such an inspiring and comforting time for me that I found it difficult to sleep that night, so I spent the greater part of the night's hours praising and thanking the Lord for past, present, and future blessings.

Once again, God gave me the desires of my heart because He knew what I needed even before I realized my need. How blessed I was, going and coming because God was preparing the way and then leading me out of grief into joy. I give Him all the praise and glory! Is this your experience when you choose to delight yourself in the Lord? Maybe you haven't delighted yourself in Him yet. Why not do so today? Then you, too, will receive the desires of your heart. "Delight yourself in the Lord and He will give you the desires of your heart" (Psalm 37: 4 NIV).

Balance

Have you ever entertained two emotions at the same time, such as joy and sorrow, excitement and anxiety, disappointment and gratitude? It seems to be quite a common human experience. On Sunday afternoon after being informed that my expected Australian guests, Conrad Boardman and Marion Carvey, were not able to travel because of the sudden onset of illness, I experienced both disappointment and gratitude. I was disappointed both for them and myself, yet at the same time, I was thankful the illness happened in their home country while they were with relatives.

Life is filled with a multitude of double-emotion events which are both powerful and challenging. It's our Christian faith that gives us equilibrium. God, in the person of the Holy Spirit, is ever reaching out and working within us to keep us in balance. To have the mind of Christ means we give thanks in all circumstances and, in so doing, are able to see the Good News in any bad news.

Beginnings

The truth is we are all terminal! Nothing lasts forever except the Word of God. That being so, now is the time to choose what is more important to us as we begin a New Year. Join me, won't you? Let's make a list of the five top issues or tasks we want to accomplish in the time ahead. Just write them down as they come to mind. Here is an example:

1. Unclutter house
2. Increase prayer time
3. Plan a party
4. Visit more friends
5. Do more Bible study

Next, let's decide which ones are most important and rank them in that order. Who knows, the one assigned as number 1 may really turn out to be number 5 after we've thought about priorities. Now that we've dreamed and prioritized, let's begin tackling that list. Here we go—let's work on number 1. Happy living of the abundant life!

Called to Worship

Well, here I am in the pew, and what a view I have! I am surrounded by beautiful architecture, by numerous symbols of the Christian faith, by living saints—believers—and by that cloud of invisible witnesses. The only word I can think of to describe my feelings is *awe*!

When I sit in the pew, I become aware that I am not alone but rather in a communal setting, similar to sitting in the bleachers at a ball game or rodeo. Yet, there is a defining difference. In the sanctuary, you and I are "sitting on the field," looking toward the empty cross which hangs on the wall above the choir loft. It is here that we look up and worship, while at the games we look down and cheer.

This view from the pew is our opportunity to worship God Almighty, our Creator and Redeemer, and, in so doing, to be inspired, transformed, and empowered. Being on the field is a calling, and God, who has called us, wants to spend time with us in His house.

By the power of His Holy Spirit, the Lord is able to grow in us the fruits He desires for us to bear: love, joy, peace, patience, kindness, goodness, faithfulness, gentleness, and self-control.

When you sit in the pew, look around, take in the architectural beauty, the symbols of our faith, the saints near you, and sense the inestimable number of invisible witnesses looking on. Remember that the Risen Lord and Savior, Jesus Christ, is present. He is awaiting our approach. Come, let us adore Him!

Change

"Excuse me, Mister, do you have change for a dollar?" Sound familiar? Change is still money; it's just money in a different form! We can be sure of one thing that will continue to occur as long as we live, and that is change! Often we decide to make changes for various reasons, and other times change comes regardless of our actions or desires. Keep in mind that birth requires change, growth depends on change, and death brings the ultimate change.

The Spirit's leading directs us to expect good things because God has promised to guide us in His ways and to bless our lives always. Let us look ahead with joy!

Circumstances

The last few weeks' happenings have brought to mind a series of statements I heard some years ago on the radio. The announcer said something like this: "We are all either going into trouble, experiencing trouble, or coming out of trouble." This should be no surprise for the Christian because Jesus gave us His counsel on the subject in John 16:33: "I have told you these things, so that in me you may have peace. In this world you will have trouble. But take heart! I have overcome the world" (NIV). I need to be reminded of this scripture daily. It helps me to deal with the three phases of trouble I am presently dealing with.

> Phase 1—Going into trouble:
> My dog, Lady, has become ill, and the diagnosis is cancer.
>
> Phase 2—Experiencing trouble:
> I have several close friends who are suffering with serious health challenges.
>
> Phase 3—Coming out of trouble:
> A lawsuit filed against my mother's estate after her death in 2000 was finally settled after nine years.

I am also reminded I need to practice an attitude of gratitude since scripture tells us to "give thanks in all circumstances, for this is God's will for you in Christ Jesus" (1 Thessalonians 5:18 NIV). I do thank God for His gracious love and kind mercy and for each one of you. I wish you God's perfect peace.

Companionship

Recently, I have been reading a book titled *May I Walk You Home?* by Melody Rossi. It deals with sharing Christ's love with the dying. I was drawn to this book by its title. I can well remember as a child being walked home by a parent or friend. I felt special and protected enjoying the company of the one who walked at my side.

Frequently in life, we may be given the unique opportunity to accompany a loved one to heaven's door. The moments shared are often some of life's most difficult and, at the same time, indescribably precious. May I encourage you to fear not but be willing to walk alongside your loved one in humble service as he or she approaches the portal to heaven. The Holy Spirit will be with you both as you walk together. For it is written, "For this God our God for ever and ever; he will be our guide even to the end" (Psalm 48:14 NIV).

May God bless you and lead you every step of the way until you deliver your loved one safely into His keeping.

Deliverance

One afternoon before Christmas, I was driving to our family home in Greenville, Mississippi, for a few days with my brother, Bill. It was after five o'clock, it was beginning to get dark, and traffic was extra-heavy. I was in the middle lane, traveling west on Highway 82 and proceeding slowly between stoplights when I saw, about three car lengths ahead of me, some articles fly off a vehicle and land in various lanes. The item that landed in the middle lane appeared to be flat, so I decided to pass slowly over it. Wrong decision! Somehow it got caught underneath my car and began to make a faint scraping sound. I knew then that I was "between a rock and a hard place" because I couldn't stop and get out with cars whizzing past on either side. I inched toward the next stoplight, and when I began to go forward again, I heard the article shift, get re-caught, and make a deafening noise. All the while I was asking the Lord to help me make it quickly to a safe place and pull out of traffic.

I continued to inch along, and the noise was frightening! Finally, I made it to the light at the intersection of Highways 82 and 1 where I turned south and got in the right lane to turn off the highway into a parking lot across from a Walgreens. As I was turning off, I saw this lady in a truck on my left motioning frantically to me. When I stopped and exited my car, she pulled alongside and pointed to the driver's door area and said, "It's right down there." Before I could respond, she jumped out of her car, dropped to the ground, and slid under my car pulling at something. At the same time, two men drove up and jumped out of their truck exclaiming, "Lady! Lady! We thought your car was going to blow up. We've never seen so many sparks!"

At that moment, the lady came up from under the car with a piece of metal about twelve inches long. She said, "There's more under there." One of the guys said, "Let me see. I'll get it." He dropped down, went under the car, and hollered back, "I can get this out with something in my truck." After getting a tool from his truck, he again went under my car, tied the tool onto the object, stood up, and gave a big yank. Out came another piece of metal the length of a yardstick! Words are really inadequate to express what I felt. Let me just say that I was overwhelmed with relief, speechless with wonder, and so thankful for being delivered from danger so quickly and totally.

My angels were three beautiful African-American young adults. We hugged, talked, and hugged again before wishing one another a "Merry Christmas." I told them that they had made Christmas come alive for me. I was reminded of the children's hymn "Jesus Loves the Little Children."

> Jesus loves the little children,
> All the children of the world.
> Red and yellow, black and white,
> They are precious in His sight.

Precious! That's how they made me feel with their concern for me and how I feel about them. God answered my prayer swiftly and lovingly through the kindness of those young people. To God be the glory!

Devotion

On July 20, I adopted a dog named Lady from a couple in Brandon, Mississippi, who were preparing to welcome a second child into their home. Lady was a five-year-old corgi-terrier mix with black and white markings. She was housebroken, socialized to other animals and small children, and responsive to specific verbal commands. I told the couple that I was convinced God engineered the whole set of circumstances with the end result being a new home for Lady. She settled in quite well, was full of energy and curiosity, was eager to please, and was quick to submit when scolded. Lady wanted to be where I was and was vigilant in keeping track of my whereabouts. She learned quickly and seemed to enjoy every new venture.

Adjusting to Lady's presence in my life caused me to think about my relationship with the Holy Spirit.

Have I settled into daily contact with Him?

Am I filled with energy and curiosity as I read His Word and hear His voice?

Am I eager to please Him?

Am I quick to submit when I sense His displeasure?

Do I desire His continual presence?

Am I vigilant in sensing His promptings in my daily life?

Do I learn quickly and take pleasure from His teachings?

If I can allow myself to become as willing, as zealous, and as devoted to my Savior as Lady was to me, I will know for sure that I am heading home on the narrow royal road.

Diligence and Discernment

Two things that have made an impression on me lately are ant beds and junk mail! Every few days a new ant bed appears somewhere in my yard. I have to be doubly vigilant when walking my dog Nick to be sure to avoid any close proximity to their mounds or problems resulting from a rapid and multiple-stinging defense system. The least nearby vibration will set off the speedy defense of their well-built mound.

The Bible tells us to "go to the ant, you sluggard; consider its ways and be wise! It has no commander, no overseer or ruler, yet it stores its provisions in summer and gathers its food at harvest" (Proverbs 6:6–8 NIV). The ant is a committed worker that toils with speed and efficiency, seemingly inner directed and keenly attuned to anything that threatens the mound. In the same way, I, as a Christian, should be committed to the work God has called me to do. I should be quick to respond to the Holy Spirit's prompting, eagerly carrying out my assignments with efficiency and with a growing ability to discern when something threatens my faith walk.

I get loads of junk mail, and the sheer repetition and volume of it gets on my last nerve! So what to do? I dump it upon receipt now. I no longer deliberate. Some things in my life are like junk mail: negative thoughts, bad ideas, painful memories, guilt, shame, blame, worry, and fear. So what to do? Surrender them to God, the Father, through Jesus, the Savior. I no longer deliberate; I kneel. What about you?

Double Blessing

Recently, after several days of continuous rain, I ventured outside during a lull to walk my dog Lady. The sky was an interesting collage of light and dark clouds. As I looked down the hill, I was surprised to see the most beautiful rainbow. I could see it almost from end to end. Its colors were so bold and vibrant as I stood transfixed, taking in the beauty of the different hues while remembering God's promise to Noah and his sons:

> I solemnly promise you and your children and the animals you brought with you—all these birds and cattle and wild animals—that I will never again send another flood to destroy the earth. And I seal this promise with this sign: I have placed my rainbow in the clouds as a sign of my promise until the end of time, to you and to all the earth. When I send clouds over the earth, the rainbow will be seen in the clouds, and I will remember my promise to you and to every being, that never again will the floods come and destroy all life. For I will see the rainbow in the cloud and remember my eternal promise to every living being on the earth. (Genesis 9:9–17 LB)

Keeping this scripture in mind, I walked to the backyard where I could see the rainbow's arc bending toward the earth and touching somewhere beyond my sight. I returned to the front yard, looked once again, and was further surprised by a second rainbow, which was equally as stunning as the first. I became overwhelmed with the realization at that moment of how generous God is to each one of us. He doesn't just bless us one time and call it quits. He blesses us over and over and over again each and every day of our lives and patiently waits for us to become aware and rejoice in His unending goodness.

What do you see today? It may be a double blessing from God's hand. Wake up and see what the Lord has prepared for you. Give Him thanks and praise for His promises!

Empowered Presence

An experience I had several nights ago started me thinking about my body being a repository of electrical energy. In fact, without the presence of this energy, my body would die. We've all heard the term *brain-dead*, which means that all electrical activity within the brain has stopped, signaling the cessation of physical life. Keep this in mind as I relate my experience.

When I retired for the evening, I left the radio in my bedroom on all night. The next morning when I awoke in the wee hours, the radio was putting out a barrage of static interspersed with music and words. I got up, and as I approached the radio, the nearer I came to it, the clearer the reception became. The energy emanating from my body stabilized and focused the station's setting.

This caused me to wonder if I, as a Christian filled with the Holy Spirit, truly realize that I am empowered by God to bring clarity into confused situations and to distracted individuals when I draw near. Scripture says that God has imparted special gifts to those who claim His Son as Savior and Lord:

> For God did not give us a spirit of timidity, but a spirit
> of power, of love, and of self discipline. (2 Timothy
> 1:7 NIV)

What a relief I felt when I could hear the music being played without any interference. Think what a difference you and I can offer to individuals who may be discouraged and overwhelmed in their daily lives. When we draw near, our *empowered presence* has the potential to bring to them the blessings of faith, hope, and love.

All you and I have to do is *acknowledge* and *accept* the Holy Spirit's *powerful presence and then allow Him to lead*. In other words, *trust* and *obey*! Are you ready? Come on! Let's begin!

Expectant Belief

Think with me, will you? When you ask God for something in prayer, do you really believe that He is listening? I do. If you do, do you actually have confidence that He will answer your prayer? I do. Here's why. God in His Word promises to answer. When I ask, believing, he will answer.

I asked God to enable me to minister in specific ways to two of my dear friends whom I've known and loved for many years. I asked Him for mercy in both their situations. God answered my pleas, and I give Him all the praise and glory!

In recent weeks I have been poised in the middle of the life passages of these two friends. One is in a hospice inpatient unit in Perry, Georgia, and the other is a hospice patient in her home in Ridgeland, Mississippi. Both have been very ill and moving toward the Lord's call to come home.

My Georgia friend, Martha Bagby Mims, died the night of March 14, 2011, but not before God allowed me several visits at her bedside to speak words of love and peace to her. She saw and heard me; she knew I was there. What a gift for both of us! Thank you, precious Lord. I wrote her eulogy while I was there, since she had asked me, over a year ago, if I would speak at her funeral. Her daughter, Lisa Bagby Lawson, read it in my absence. So I did speak, just not in the way I thought I would. Prayer requests one and two were answered. The first was for power to minister and the second was for God's mercy.

My Ridgeland friend, JuJu Crittenden, whose condition has been changing these last weeks, longed to see our mutual childhood friend, Florence St. John, who now lives in the Washington, DC, area. When she was approximately eleven years old, JuJu was a flower girl in Florence's wedding. It has been many years since they have seen each other. Two days after returning from the Georgia trip, I was off to Jackson, Mississippi, to meet Florence's plane and then stay with her a few nights in a hotel to transport her back and forth to JuJu's home. The reunion was ever so sweet, and their visit that first day was above and beyond all I had envisioned. The days that have followed their time together find JuJu in a weakening condition. God's timing is always perfect. Thank you, Lord.

Experiencing Holiness

I recall a song from my younger years titled "Moments to Remember," performed by The Four Lads. It's a beautiful tune, and when I hear it, my mind is flooded with happy memories of my youth.

Bible Sunday 2008, an annual celebration of God's Word begun by the American Bible Society in 1915, is now a collection of moments to remember. In the quiet of the church parlor before the service that Sunday, cast members gathered in costumes and formed a circle at my request. They were asked to extend their hands for anointing as I prayed for each individual by name: "Be anointed ___ by the power of the Holy Spirit to bear witness this day to the Lord Jesus Christ, the Living Word."

As I rounded the circle, I could barely speak as it was such a moment of precious holiness—the quiet, the reverence, and the glow on each dear face before me as we surrendered to the presence of the Holy Spirit. I shall long remember those soul-stirring moments and the magnificent worship experience that followed. Truly, the Lord was glorified in His temple that Sunday.

Faith Signposts

The first week of August, I traveled with my brother, Bill, to his son's home in Thomaston, Georgia, to celebrate two birthdays in our family. Bill did the driving while I busied myself by working crosswords and looking at the passing scenery. As we journeyed along, I began to pay particular attention to any signs of the Christian faith: Bethlehem Creek, King's Pasture Church, Lone Pilgrim Church, and so forth. As we approached Demopolis, Alabama, we had to come to a full stop and await our turn to pass through a section of highway construction. Before long, a truck approached that was leading a line of cars toward us from the opposite direction in the one free lane. The truck turned around as the cars went on their way, and then the truck began to lead us through the construction area. Guess what the sign on the truck said? Pilot Car—Follow Me.

Wow! Talk about a sign of faith! How about a direct message from the Savior! Did Jesus not say, "I am the Way, the Truth, and the Life" (John 14:6 NIV)? When you are out and about this week, look around and take notice of the many signs of our faith. They're everywhere if you use your spiritual eyes.

For the Love of Nick

After the death of my dog, Lady, in November, I decided to grieve awhile and then consider adopting another dog. In January, I went to CARA, the Community Animal Rescue and Adoption shelter in Jackson, Mississippi, to look at some dogs I had viewed on their website. None of the ones I had asked to see were the right fit for me. Then the director brought in this little white dog named Nick. He was very friendly, and before I left, he had fallen asleep between my feet while I sat and waited to speak to the director. All I can say is from that moment on I was hooked and thus began the process to give Nick a home.

On February 17, 2010, I picked Nick up from CARA, and after a brief stopover at my friend JuJu's in Ridgeland, Mississippi, the two of us headed to Kosciusko. My home has become his, and he has adopted me. What fun! I delight in watching his antics with his rawhide bone and his toys. He is such a happy little fellow and likes to bound into my lap for petting and play. He never meets a stranger and enjoys the affectionate attention of my outside cat, Surprise. I have taken him to both the family home in Greenville and the lake house in Oxford only to find him a quick study in adaptability. He likes to ride in the car either in the front seat, for a short hop, or in his carrier in the back where he contentedly chews his bone and then naps.

I adopted him knowing that he had heartworms, and so far he has done well during treatment. We have a few more miles to go in his recovery, but the good end is in sight. My heart is full of thanksgiving for the pleasure Nick has added to my daily life. I rescued him, and he has returned the favor.

Isn't that what we really are called to do for one another in our relationships? We save each other with our prayers, our presence, our gifts, our sharing of laughter and tears, and our loving concern expressed in a thousand different ways. Acting this way by the power of the Holy Spirit drives away gloom and despair from our lives and allows Him to produce hope in our hearts. The next time someone comes to you for comfort, sweep that person into an encouraging hug for both your sakes. I invite you to join me today in reading 1 Corinthians 13, the love chapter, and allowing the Holy Spirit to fill you with His transforming love every day.

Fruit Bearers

> Such knowledge is too wonderful for me, too lofty
> for me to attain. Where can I go from Your Spirit?
> Where can I flee from your presence? If I go up to
> the heavens, you are there; if I make my bed in the
> depths, you are there. If I rise on the wings of dawn,
> if I settle on the far side of the sea, even there your
> hand will guide me, your right hand will hold me fast
> (Psalm 139:6–10 NIV).

A week ago, while walking in my front yard, I noticed on the left side of the house a large bush laden down with dark red camellia blossoms. I counted ten flowers on one major branch. I checked again this week and it continues to produce more and more blooms.

Seeing them caused me to reflect on God's design in every facet of creation: plants, animals, birds, fish, and humans. We are all created to produce fruit. In our case, God enables us to produce both physical and spiritual fruit.

I recall a family road trip to California in the 1950s during which I saw flowers blooming in the Arizona desert. In 1963, while in the Swiss Alps, I stood at the tundra line where at my feet were tiny exquisite blooms rising out of the iced-over soil. In my yard today, a forsythia bush is putting forth its yellow plumage while wee purple blossoms are coming up in the lawn between blades of brown and green grass.

In my own life, I remember times of great sadness that produced in me some fruit of the Spirit—kindness and gentleness. Then there were those seasons of great well-being and gladness that produced other fruits—generosity and self-control.

All the seasons of our lives are intended to enable us to bear the fruit that the Holy Spirit wishes to grow in us. Even in the most rugged or unlikely circumstances, God's Spirit is able to care for us and do His work in and through our lives. God is always with us. He gives us His Spirit, and if we will allow Him to work, He will produce fruit—extraordinary and supernatural fruit—in our lives and then ask us to lift it up for all to see His handiwork.

> But the fruit of the Spirit is love, joy, peace, patience, kindness, goodness, faithfulness, gentleness and self-control. Against such things there is no law (Galatians 5:22–23 NIV).

Walk around in your yard or over your property. What do you see? Look within your own heart, and behold, the Holy Spirit is at work in your life to enable you to bear the wondrous fruit that tells the world that you belong to Jesus Christ, the Creator and Redeemer of planet earth.

Good-byes

"God Be with You till We Meet Again"—I've always liked this hymn by Jeremiah Rankin (1882). The lyrics are a prayer of blessing on those we love when times of separation come. This is one of those times in my personal life and in our church life.

I'll never forget the day that the new pastor, Rev. James Salter, swept into my life and to the bedside of my friend, Diamond Brown, only weeks before the Lord called her home. God answered my earnest prayer that day by sending to us this man of God whose heart was like his Master's—kind and compassionate. James swept into our lives at a time of crisis, and we both were forever changed.

So, we love and we lose. Actually, that is the rhythm of life. Whether it's when children first begin school, their graduation day, leaving for college, serving our country, starting their own family, or taking a new job in another locale, we have to say good-bye for a time. Then there are the good-byes when our earthly lives are finished and we enter the new existence God has prepared for us. Loving and losing—loving and losing.

The wonderful promise of God is that in all our days, He goes before us to form His will for us. He cares for those we leave behind and tells us that His plans for each of us are special and custom designed. If we ask Him, He will show us what is in His mind.

As James Salter and his wife, Tricia, and family leave Kosciusko, Mississippi, to answer God's call in Gautier, Mississippi, let us give thanks for their time of ministry with us and let us continue to pray for them in the days and months ahead. We truly have been blessed that God sent them our way.

May God be with you till we meet again.

Home

Going home:

> After school,
> From the doctor's office,
> From camp,
> After the ball game,
> After the prom,
> After church,
> From vacation,
> From college,
> After the wedding,
> After the party,
> After the funeral,
> After work,
> From the store,
> From the hospital—

it's always good to get home! Don't you agree? Think what it will be like to return to your eternal home one day when your life's work is done. It will be wonderful to walk into your heavenly home into the arms of your Risen Savior, Jesus, who has prepared a place just for you! Thank Him today for His promise to you and your family.

Identity

Have you heard the expression "It's all in a name"? I began thinking about that phrase and how significant names are. We each have a name, usually bestowed on us at birth by our parents, and some even have nicknames affectionately used over a lifetime by family and friends. We also call things, places, and experiences by name. I was struck by how important and distinctive the naming process is.

Scripture underscores this truth that words have power and that one particular name is all powerful—Jesus! Mary and Joseph were informed by the angel Gabriel that God the Father had decreed that the baby Mary would deliver was to be named Jesus (Matthew 1:2). The man named Jesus became a magnet in his thirty years of earthly ministry drawing both praise and derision. His name brings the same result in our world today just as He told His disciples it would.

The name of Jesus is like no other name. It is full of wonder-working, transforming power, and for this reason, the world fears it and seeks to shut down its use. Since we bear His name and claim Him as Savior, Lord, and King, I invite you to join me in a brief study that will increase your understanding of what the Holy Scripture teaches about His name: Matthew 1:21, Matthew 18:20, John 16:23–24, Acts 4:12, Romans 10:13, Philippians 2:9–10, and Colossians 3:17.

Now, after reading these references, we can truly say it's all in His name: salvation, deliverance, healing, forgiveness, authority, provision, resurrection, and eternal life. Glory to God! This, my dear friends, is our identity—we who claim the name of Jesus. May God be praised!

Illumination

The other afternoon, I was sitting on the sofa in the den and looked up. My eyes were immediately drawn to the far wall where the bright rays of sunlight were streaming through the backdoor and illuminating the wallpaper. Every smooth and rough place was exposed. As the beams slowly inched across the wall, they fell upon this beautiful oil painting of an East Indian woman, which was painted many years ago by my dear friend, Diamond Brown. The hues on the canvas became vibrant, and the colorful figure was transformed right before my very eyes. Wow!

It seems to me that life is like this for each one of us. Every day we are moving through our earthly lives more rapidly than we often realize except in those moments when we are startled by some event. It is then that we comprehend that life is, indeed, very brief. The second insight, in addition to life's brevity, is what a difference light makes in a dark place. Light restores our vision so we can see not only the beauty around us and the beauty in others but also the dangers and hazards that lie before us.

We, as Christians, are called to be "bearers of the Christ Light." We are to witness to the Risen Lord, who said, "I am the light of the world" (John 8:12 NIV). His light expels darkness and brings deliverance to anyone stumbling in the dark. We are enabled to burn brightly by keeping our lights trimmed through daily confession, repentance, prayer, and studying the written Word of God.

Thinking on these two truths, let us ask the Holy Spirit to turn up the light in each of our lives and empower us to make every precious second of our earthly life to reflect His wondrous light into the darkness of this world.

Recommended scriptures for study are: 2 Samuel 22:29, Psalm 119:105, 2 Corinthians 4:6, 1 John 1:7.

In His Name

Christians have been dubbed "Easter People"! What is the significance of such a title? It is a vivid reminder that in Christ we are

Chosen,
Called,
Saved,
Forgiven,
Set Apart,
Filled,
Gifted,
Clothed with Power.

We are witnesses to the Good News that Jesus, the Messiah, the Son of God, is risen from the dead, and He is with us, by the power of the Holy Spirit, in our daily walk of faith.

Rejoice, Christians! Let us continue with our Risen Lord in worship and witness.

Journey of Joy

Trouble came our way, we lived with it for many a day, and then we left it and walked away. This was the journey I took with my precious dog, Lady. We enjoyed a very brief, yet deeply sweet, relationship. Unsought, she came into my life and filled it up to overflowing. Then my love for her demanded a quick, gentle good-bye in November of 2009. I grieved, and I rejoiced.

She was the perfect pet companion. Our days together were so pleasurable, full of fun, adventure, and closeness. As Goldilocks said, "Just right!" I was broken, sad, and empty. Yet at the same time, I was healing. I became content in my grief and more open to the inner workings of the Holy Spirit.

Lady came into my life, saw me, and loved me. She conquered my heart, and my life has been forever changed. Thank you, gracious God, for my time with Lady. "The Lord is close to the brokenhearted and saves those who are crushed in spirit" (Psalm 34:18 NIV).

Joy Shines Through

Have you ever felt as if you were on an emotional roller coaster? I have. Let me share with you what I'm talking about. One March morning, while reading the Jackson, Mississippi, newspaper the *Clarion-Ledger*, I was stunned and saddened to see the obituary of my Kappa Delta sorority big sister, Patricia McRaney Hootsell (1939–2011). I had been in touch with her by mail in recent years but longed to see her again before summer's end. I had not seen her since college days. Alas, I was too late.

Enter *Shock—Grief—Regret*—followed by *Joy*!

On Friday, April 15, 2011 I received the news of JuJu's death in Ridgeland. A precious historical voice had become silent.

Enter *Sadness—Relief*—followed by *Joy*!

Later the same morning my phone rang. I heard from Janice

Contini, a dear friend from seminary days. I had lost contact with her and had prayed, asking God to help me find her. He did.

Enter *Surprise—Pleasure*—followed by *Joy*!

All of my life, I've experienced the ups and downs of my emotional reactions to life's events. I recall that God's Holy Word in the book of Ecclesiastes 3:1 says, "There is a time for everything, and a season for every activity under heaven" (NIV). Though my emotions may behave at times like mercury in a thermometer, my faith in God and His Word is the bedrock that gives my life stability. I know that come what may, God goes before me to prepare the way. His Holy Spirit indwells me all the time and ministers to my every need. "Surely goodness and love will follow me all the days of my life and I will dwell in the house of the Lord forever" (Psalm 23:6 NIV).

Enter *Faith—Hope—Love*—followed by *Joy*—resulting in *Peace*!

May you, like I, have the blessed assurance of knowing with absolute certainty that when emotions wax and wane, you are held in protective custody by your heavenly Father. He is a wonderful God!

Looking Back

I have been asked to write an article about myself for the 1959 Greenville High School class reunion, which is scheduled for the weekend of October 23, 2009. The question posted on the reunion's website was "What have you been doing for the last fifty years?" My, my, that's one inquiry that will make a person think, and think, and think again!

Can it really be that many years ago? Sometimes it seems like only yesterday that I was on the football field leading cheers for the Greenville High School Hornets; going to dances; doing homework; taking exams; working on copy for the *Vespa*, our school yearbook; talking on the telephone about the latest teen scoop; learning my lines for the senior play; and planning for graduation and college. Yet it's been fifty years since I donned that cap and gown and marched down the aisle to receive that hard-earned diploma. All this just goes to prove the truth of the phrase, "Tempus fugit" (time flies), and that it does, my friends.

Since high school, I've been learning, struggling, and growing while attending college, seminary, graduate school, and working in a variety of schools, hospitals, and churches. I've met wonderful and interesting individuals in the places I've lived, sometimes on the job and other times during worship and fellowship and even in the halls and rooms of hospitals. I've taught and counseled with countless children, young people, and adults from all types of backgrounds. I've studied and prayed and cried and laughed. I've buried my parents and several close friends as well as a number of precious pets.

I've been well and hearty, young and foolish, on the mountaintop and in the valley. I've been sick and weak, fearful and brave, you name it, and I've been there at some point in these last fifty years. Yet through every day of that time span, the One constantly beside me has been God's Holy Spirit, loving me when I was unlovable, waiting for me when I was resistant or reluctant or rebellious, encouraging me when I was hesitant, comforting me when I was sad, and all the time, gently, yet firmly, leading me along the path of righteousness.

I've been many places, known lots of people, and participated in a myriad of different experiences, events, and relationships. Each place, each individual, each experience, each event, and each relationship has been used by God to bring me nearer to Him. Now, He has my full attention; it's high time, don't you agree? Maybe you could benefit from asking yourself an adaptation of this same question. Just fill in the blank. What have you been doing for the last ___ years?

Moving On

One day recently, as I was driving down Jefferson Street, my attention was drawn to an attractive house with a "For Sale" sign in the yard. The dwelling was blatantly empty, as there were no signs of life there.

I began to think of how similar a vacant house is to the death of an individual. When I die ... my spirit, which will never die, will exit my earthly body and be transported into the presence of God. There will be no signs of life in my remains. I will have moved on, and one day, I will be given a new imperishable covering or body for my spirit.

This reality about the body after death became starkly clear to me in 1972, at the time of my maternal grandmother's passing. I drove to my parents' home from my residence in New Orleans and discovered friends and neighbors taking care of things at their home while my parents were at the funeral home.

I walked into the utility room and saw my grandmother's overnight case. Laid out on the ironing board were the following items: her eyeglasses, car and house keys, wallet, credit cards, driver's license, comb, brush, lipstick and compact, and several other items. Seeing all those things made me realize that she no longer needed any of them because she was no longer alive on earth. She had moved on.

At the funeral home, I went up to the casket and, while I recognized her body by its outward appearance and the clothes that adorned it, she wasn't present. That unique spirit that had animated her body was gone. She had moved on.

Dying is like moving. You leave one house and move into a different one. You leave one location and move to a new one. For the Christian, dying is stepping through a doorway into a new dimension that is illuminated by the Holy Presence of Jesus Christ. What a move that will be!

Rejoice, O Christian! The best is yet to be ... for you and I ... are bound for glory in eternity.

New Insights

Several weeks ago, I experienced two moments of enhanced spiritual awareness while in attendance at separate events. The first occurred while attending the memorial service of a friend. I sat behind a young couple with their two little girls in tow. The oldest, a pretty blond, sat on the pew between her parents while the youngest, a beautiful dark-haired wee girl with big brown eyes and creamy-colored skin, was nestled snugly in her father's arms. She looked around wide-eyed at all the people and then, turning to her daddy, took her free hand and ever so gently stroked his cheek. When he looked at her adoringly, she gave him a brilliant smile. Then, taking a firmer grip on his upper arm with one hand and circling his neck with her other hand, she laid her head down on his shoulder looking totally at peace and secure in her daddy's embrace.

Wow! What a picture of my relationship with my heavenly Father! As I witnessed their exchange, my eyes began to fill with tears from the sheer beauty of their bond of love—a mystery of God's making. I became keenly aware in an instant that clinging to God and resting in His gently strong embrace is my only true place of peace and security in this life.

In another small group gathering that I was privileged to attend, I watched an exceptionally pretty young mother of an adorable infant lovingly attend to her daughter's every need. I was mesmerized by the incredible bond between them, the closeness, the intuitive insight of the mother, and the delight they both experienced in each others' company.

Wow! Once again I saw and understood the pleasure that God takes in being with me, His child, created in His image. He longs for fellowship with me so He can tend to my every need and share His Word with me, which, in turn, creates His life in me where only death once reigned

His embrace is beyond compare, and His voice is tender and

winsome. Can you hear Him? He is calling for you, yes, you! He wants you to come and sit with Him awhile and let Him love you. I promise you will find rest for your soul. Won't you come now? He's waiting, waiting just for you.

New Life

Today as I looked into my backyard, I saw green sprouts shooting up and out of the ground and early bloomers greeting me from one flower bed. What only yesterday appeared dead and barren today is alive and fruitful.

I thought about my heart—my spiritual life. Do I seem dead and barren to those around me? Is the Holy Spirit causing new growth to blossom—new areas of understanding and fresh offerings of love and mercy—the beginnings of His Word becoming flesh in me? I pray it is so, not only in my life but also in yours.

God's peace to you and your family this holy season.

Our Destiny

In Christ, we are

    chosen,
    called,
    saved,
    forgiven,
    set apart,
    filled,
    gifted,
    empowered—

    to tell the story of Jesus and His love everyday in any circumstance.
Rejoice, for the Lord goes before us to prepare the way!

Priorities

There's a song from the musical *Oliver!*, which I saw on Broadway many years ago. It begins, "I am reviewing the situation ..." That's what I've been doing this the first month of the New Year—rethinking my priorities.

What matters to me? What action am I going to take in regard to those things that matter the most? These are good questions and ones I needed to ask and answer.

After some thinking and praying, I made a list that includes eight projects that matter to me and need to be done by me. Several will be solo endeavors while others will require assistance from friends or professionals who possess skills that I do not have.

I recall the saying "If you keep doing something the same way, you'll get the same result." Therefore, it follows that If I do something a different way, the result will be different! I am going to be putting that truth into practice. In fact, I am already out of the starting gate and on project 1: The reworking of my extensive book collection.

The other projects I have named include the following: preparing a body of written work to be published, arranging selected T-shirts in a pattern to be made into a quilt, collating and filing business documents, beginning to organize a collection of sermon excerpts into book form, planning visits to special places to see friends and family, cleaning out clothes closets, gathering tax data, and reworking the order and contents of the utility room. Whew! This is some list I've made for myself.

I had a list last year, and some of the projects were accomplished in a manner beyond my expectation while others did not bring the result I had hoped for. That's all part of resetting and executing priorities. The good news is that the Holy Spirit will help me to accomplish whatever is in line with the Father's will.

My plan of action in this New Year is based on the scripture from

2 Corinthians 5:17: "Therefore, if anyone is in Christ, he is a new creation; the old is gone, the new has come!" (NIV).

Have you made your list yet? Why not get started today? Join me in this great adventure. Let us rejoice in the Lord for He will do great and wonderful things through us. All He requires is our willingness to allow His Spirit to work. I'm willing! Are you?

Protective Obedience

Recently, I was sitting in my car in the Sunflower store parking lot, preparing to leave when suddenly cars converged from all directions. The result was a traffic jam, and each car was brought to an abrupt stop. Each driver had been driving as if he or she was the only one in the lot, ignoring parking space lines and traffic flow indicators. I plead guilty to have done this very thing several times but not without misgivings.

As I sat there and observed, I thought back to my early years of driving and recalled that such sights were not much in practice back then. Drivers pretty well stayed in their correct lanes and were predictable when seeking a parking space. Perhaps today's "no holds barred" driving is a symptom of a society that has grown less careful and more selfish—each person doing what is right in his or her own sight.

If we remember, God has given us laws to live by. He did so to protect us and to produce blessings in our lives. Just as the traffic laws are in place to protect us and to allow safe movement from one area to another, I was brought into line by the Holy Spirit as I sat there that day. Those misgivings I mentioned earlier had been the Holy Spirit telling me that my driving needed to be not just for my needs, but for the other person's as well—no shortcuts allowed that could endanger my neighbor or me. After all, if we profess Christ, each person is our neighbor and we are to serve those neighbors with our best of everything, which includes driving carefully and thoughtfully. So what we do in the parking lot matters!

Purification

Let it snow, let it snow, let it snow! And it did! Wasn't it beautiful? I was entranced watching it fall and mesmerized when I looked out on a totally white landscape. Everything was covered, and there was no sound, just stillness and brilliance. This brought to mind several lines from "'Twas the Night Before Christmas."

The moon on the breast of the new fallen snow
Gave the luster of midday to objects below.

Then I thought of this scripture from Isaiah that speaks of the gracious gift of salvation God offers through His grace to those who believe.

> Come now, let us reason together, says the Lord.
> Though your sins be as scarlet, they shall be as white
> as snow... (Isaiah 1:18 NIV).

My last impression was how fresh and clean the air becomes after a snowfall. I took some deep breaths of that cold clean air and felt refreshed and energized. Clean and fresh—that's how we are as new creatures having been washed in the blood of the Lamb which makes us ready for holy living and sweet fellowship with our Lord. This is the ultimate change made possible through the blood of the Lamb at Calvary. All glory to the Lord, Jesus Christ!

Let us come before Him today with penitent hearts and receive His generous gift of total forgiveness. We will come forth brilliantly white and fresh with the stillness within that only our Savior can bestow. Alleluia! Alleluia! May God be praised!

Rebirth

"Born again, there's really been a change in me. Born again, just like Jesus said ..." In the words of the song, we've been born again, right? This means we've been washed in the blood of the Lamb of God whose name is Jesus. When God, the Father, looks at us, He sees the righteousness of His Son, Jesus Christ. Though our sins were red as crimson, now we are washed white as snow and covered by the glistening garment of Christ.

Actually, it's as if we never ever sinned—that's what justification is. When we were lost (unregenerate), we were insensitive to the things of God. In reality, we were in the dark. But when we received Christ, we became saved (regenerate). We were found, and now we walk in the light. We are forgiven of our sins and restored to our relationship with God. Now we have peace with our heavenly Father. At this very moment, we are being recreated by the renewing or our minds toward spiritual things by the power of the Holy Spirit.

Rejoice! Let us enjoy our lives as Christians. Jesus came to give each of us an abundant life. Let's claim it today!

Reinvestment

Today I was in my front bedroom looking out the window. I saw the American flag across the street flapping in the wind as the trees behind it swayed too and fro. The sky was blue with many clouds interspersed. The fruit trees in my front yard stood plainly bare, but buds were forming. The swing on my front porch was slowly moving back and forth as cars passed by at intervals on their daily routes.

I sat at my computer hoping for an e-mail from the director of the Community Animal Rescue and Adoption shelter in Jackson, Mississippi. About a month ago, I visited there to look at several dogs that I took a liking to on the Internet with the idea of possibly adopting one. The dogs I had chosen online were not the right fit, but then, the director brought one in that stole my heart right then and there. His name was Nick, a three-year-old Maltese. I filled out the papers and, over the past weeks, I've been anxiously waiting while he's been checked over by the vet who serves the shelter, given all the shots and tests they require, and at the same time checking me out as a potential owner.

The word came today in response to my afternoon phone call that I can pick Nick up this Wednesday afternoon, February 17, 2010. The waiting is almost over. I'm excited and a little nervous because I'm making another commitment. I'm taking a chance on love, knowing, oh so well, the joy and the pain that can be involved. Yet because both of my former beloved pets, Mi-Ling, a Lhasa Apso and Lady, taught me love lessons I never knew, but now I do, so the learning for me must go on.

Look around you and see the beauty of God's creation. Listen and you, too, will hear His still, small voice calling you to commit and take another chance on love—His kind of love. "This is the day the Lord has made; let us rejoice and be glad in it" (Psalm 118:24 NIV).

Relationships

May I share a prayer that I recently uncovered when I was going through some old papers and files? It harks back to when I was on staff at Rock Spring Presbyterian Church, Atlanta, Georgia. I clipped the prayer out of the church bulletin for my treasure chest. It was written by my former colleague, the late Rev. Richard Ribble, a great and gifted man of God. It seems to me that this prayer expresses what we as Christians should be up and doing in the dawning of each new day:

> O God, we give thanks for the life and love we find in relationships. We pray for others, and thereby touch them with our thoughts: ill people who know what it is to hurt and to be afraid, lonely people who know what it is to hunger for someone's concern, pressured people who fear they are going to crack. As we think upon those whom we know and touch them with our thoughts, help us to whatever extent we can, to touch them with our lives and give us a fuller measure of the living, healing Spirit of Jesus Christ. Amen.

Reunion

As I was thinking about this article, an old saying came to mind, "Make new friends but keep the old; one is silver and the other gold." Back in 1966, I began a job in Brunswick, Georgia, teaching girls' physical education at Glynn Academy, a public high school. Along came my co-teacher, Sandra Gail Kennedy, who was a Georgia native and a recent university graduate. We both enjoyed our teaching duties and living in the beautiful coastal town of Brunswick.

In 1969, we both moved on to new challenges. I went to New Orleans, Louisiana, to teach physical education at a school in St. Bernard Parish, and Sandra entered Southwestern Baptist Theological Seminary in Fort Worth, Texas. Many years intervened before I caught up with her again this October in Augusta, Georgia. On that October day, I walked up to her in the Honey from the Rock Café, one of the exciting ministries of the Whole Life Church of which she is the founder and senior pastor. Diane Grey, who accompanied me on this great faith adventure, said that when Sandra finally realized who I was, the expression on her face was priceless! It had been forty-one years since we had last seen each other. She was beside herself! It looked as if she was going to throw her food tray in the air. She was so excited, and so was I. It was truly a God-given moment.

Our time there was amazing. The Whole Life Church is a nondenominational and multicultural fellowship that occupies an entire shopping center complex and houses several different ministries. Diane and I visited the administrative offices, the book store, the fellowship hall, the chapel, and the café. We saw the main sanctuary during our private visit with Sandra and during the Friday night Healing Explosion service. Next we toured the Freedom Center, an area set aside for dealing with deliverance from addictions, and finally the Healing Center, which offers Bible teaching on healing and healing teams available to minister to seriously ill individuals. We were privileged to hear Dr. Kennedy preach at two services and were treated royally with special seating as well as a long personal visit with her after the Thursday night service. What wonderful friends God gave me in Sandra and Diane.

I deeply desired to find Sandra. God answered my prayer. He showered both Diane and me with His wonderful truth and love while we were at the Whole Life Church. To God be the glory! "Delight yourself in the Lord and he will give you the desires of your heart" (Psalm 37:4 NIV). If you would like to see and hear my friend, Dr. Kennedy, check out her ministry at www.sandrakennedy.org or www.wholelife.org.

Second Sight

Have you ever observed something you've looked at before and then quite suddenly see it in a new light? That's the experience I have each year during Holy Week as I watch the annual passion play production, *His Last Days*, performed by members of the Kosciusko First United Methodist Church.

Witnessing the historical reenactment of the final events in Jesus' earthly life right before my eyes is always a spiritually quickening experience.

The first time I attended in 1994, I was amazed at the exceptional quality of the production given the size of the church and the town in which it was located. Every element from the costuming to the staging and the acting was superb. I was very deeply moved that first year, and in the years that have followed, I never failed to receive what I call "second sight," which is simply a more profound understanding of the sacrifice Jesus made on the cross for you and me.

I have viewed the play as a spectator and also as a cast member. Each time, without exception, I have been touched deep in my spirit by God's unstoppable, redeeming love.

Oh yes, dear friends ...

O how He loves you and me,
He gave His life, what more could He give?
O how He loves you, O how He loves me,
O how He loves you and me.

Come and rejoice! Let us be filled with gratitude for God's gracious gift of salvation through Jesus Christ, our Savior and Risen Lord! Alleluia!

Spiritual Accounting

Dear saints, as we walk the way of the cross, let us remember those who have been beside us in the past. Their presence is warm and uplifting. As we remember the wounds of our past, let us grieve that we caused them by our sinful nature and choices. As we repent of our willfulness, let us kneel at the foot of the cross and let the blood of Jesus cleanse our lives. As we mourn His death with broken hearts, let us look with tearful eyes as we approach the tomb.

Can it be? The stone is rolled away! As we stand in awe, we receive the news, the Good News! "He is not here. He is risen and goes before you!"

Spiritual Hunger

One Sunday while in Oxford at our lake cottage, I was entering the shower when I caught my second toe in the grid of the glass shower door. Oweee! Did that hurt! I did go on and complete my shower carefully, avoiding the danger zone as I exited. I dressed for church putting on some knee-high stockings and a pair of canvas sneakers. When I put my foot down to walk, the pain was so sharp that I knew I needed to wear a different shoe if I planned on anything resembling a normal gait. First, I iced the toe and then used clear wrapping tape to anchor the injured toe to the big toe and the third toe. I pulled on a thick white sock and, finally, my tennis shoes. I stood up and took one step and then another with almost a normal gait. Yipee! Victory!

As Bill, Susan and I began the seventeen-mile drive out through the beautiful countryside to Sand Spring Presbyterian Church at Orwood, a community southwest of Oxford, Mississippi, I thought about why going to church on Sunday was so important to me. Yes, I wanted to spend time with my brother, Bill, and my nephew's wife, Susan, and I looked forward to seeing the folks at Sand Spring, but there was more. I longed to hear the Word preached by Rev. Wayne Sheffield, share my prayer concerns with his wife, Sherri, and fellowship over lunch with the Sand Spring saints. As a matter of fact, it dawned on me that I not only wanted to be there but needed to be there.

Being involved in the Body of Christ has been my most regular habit over the last sixty-eight years. I recalled years of growing up in the First Presbyterian Church in Greenville, Mississippi; my assignment to Madison Avenue Presbyterian Church and First Presbyterian Church while at seminary in New York; being a member of the First Presbyterian Church in Brunswick, Georgia, and the St. Charles Presbyterian Church in New Orleans, Louisiana; my years on staff at St. Simons Presbyterian Church, St. Simons Island, Georgia, and Rock Spring Presbyterian Church, Atlanta, Georgia; and my wonderful years here in the fellowship with the saints at Kosciusko First United Methodist Church in Kosciusko, Mississippi.

Is it any surprise then that I would yearn for this spiritual food that I am so in the habit of receiving? What does all of this lead me to conclude? None other than this simple truth: a hunger for God's Word has been growing in me since my infant baptism. It is the only hunger that truly brings fulfillment and joy. Jesus said, "I am the bread of life. He who comes to me will never go hungry, and he who believes in me will never be thirsty" (John 6:35 NIV). Are you hungry? Come, fellow believer, and feed on His all-sufficient Word.

Summer

A time to

relax,
refresh,
renew,
review,
reunite,
regroup,
rethink,
repent,
recreate,
reveal,
reconcile,
read,
reconsider,
reconnect—

but most of all a time to rejoice, for our Savior is risen and goes before us. Shalom!

Teamwork

I have been outside admiring the new roof on my house. The roofing team from A Perfect Paint in Durant, Mississippi, under the leadership of Rev. Amos Hightower, began on Monday morning, June 14, 2010 and finished Wednesday afternoon, June 16. It was a marvel to watch them take off the old roof and then put on the new one. It was hard physical labor requiring knowledge, skill, stamina, and true teamwork in the hottest of temperatures.

Each man knew his job and performed it well. When one man needed help, he called to another who promptly responded to his request and gave the assistance needed. Their ability to work well together was the vital secret of their success because even having the knowledge and skill at a task isn't enough if you can't work together to produce an excellent result. Thanks to their expertise and team ability, I have a beautiful and correctly installed roof.

Having seen their superb demonstration of working together, I thought back to experiences in my life where being a member of a team required such unity of skill and purpose. I recall being a member of a cheerleading squad, a dance class, a glee club, a camp counseling staff, church and seminary choirs, school staffs, a mental health board, church boards and committees, dramatic productions, and so forth. They were all valuable experiences for me, being a part of something bigger than myself and having a part in achieving a greater good.

This whole experience of teamwork has led me to ponder the analogy given in the Bible about the church being the Body of Christ and each one of us, a part of that body. We look at our own physical bodies and think of what it's like when we have a back problem or an injured hand. Things are harder to do because a part of our body can't perform its job to the optimum. Hence, the body's teamwork is compromised.

The same is the case when we fail to use our gifts of the Spirit when needed in our church's life. Some can teach; others can prophesy, encourage, serve, lead, or contribute to the needs of others. When used all together, the church is like an orchestra with many different instruments being played at the same time, yet it's the same piece of music led by one accomplished conductor.

Pick up your instrument, your gift. The conductor, Jesus Christ, has raised his baton. Now play the composition He has written. It's the most beautiful love song you'll ever hear! Maybe, just maybe, His love song played through us will reach the ears and heart of a lost soul.

Thanksgiving

November is the time when families regroup, reunite, and rejoice. It is the time of gathering in and gathering around each other for warmth, encouragement, and the sharing of joys and sorrows as well as hopes and dreams.

It is the time to join together in great thanksgiving to our gracious heavenly Father for giving us the blessing of each other, the wonder of family.

The Light Behind and Within

The first week of November, my brother and I traveled to see his grandson, Aaron, suited out for his school's last football game. It was a wonderful time of the year to travel seeing the breathtaking colors of autumn's leaves. All in all, we had a safe and enjoyable trip over to Thomaston, Georgia, and back to Kosciusko, Mississippi.

On the afternoon of our return trip, as Bill drove us closer and closer to our home destination, I was fascinated by the variety of clouds in the sky. I became mesmerized watching the light—the incredibly brilliant, dazzling, blinding light around their edges signaling that any break in them would result in light streaming through all the way down to the earth. The visible surface of so many of the clouds was gray, sort of dirty looking, which made me think of sin and how it soils us.

Sometimes the problems we face are like big, dark clouds overhead, yet behind those clouds is the purifying light of God's Savior Son. He is just waiting for us to call His name, and then His glorious redeeming light breaks through, transforming our situation in some unexpected way. May God be praised!

The Recovery Room

I've been in surgical recovery rooms numerous times in my life and have on several occasions, as a counselor, graduate student, and friend, visited centers designed to help persons recover from addictions. However, I've spent more of my time in the spiritual recovery room, the church, than any other place. I'm a recovering sinner washed clean by the blood of the Lamb, walking in the Spirit, feeding on the Word of God, and trusting in the finished work of the Lord Jesus Christ.

As we enter the Advent season, let us look up to the One who came as a babe to Bethlehem to save the world from sin. It is He who will give us light! The church with Christ as its head is the hospital where sinners can come to confess their sin and receive forgiveness, healing, and restoration. What a recovery plan! May God be praised!

The Secret

By the time you receive this, the "official calendar" Christmas season will have passed and a brand-new year begun. This brings to mind the lyrics from a Christmas song titled "The Secret of Christmas." It boldly proclaims the truth of what our daily lives should be like as Christians. One of the lines spells it out as follows: "It's not the things you do at Christmas time but the Christmas things you do all year through." This leads to the question, What are the "Christmas things"?

We realize, after some thought, that the "Christmas things" are hope, love, joy, and peace. These are possible because of the Holy Spirit within each one of us. If we allow Him to fill us with His hope, His love, His joy, and His peace, then we are empowered to express these gifts in innumerable ways in our daily lives.

To be specific, we carry the secret of Christmas around inside of us all the time. So let's keep on sharing with others these precious "Christmas things" and let's do it every chance we get and give God the glory!

The Shepherd's Comfort

After attending the funeral of a dear family member in Clinton, Mississippi, I began thinking this week about how to give and receive comfort. On this same day, two other friends of mine were being laid to rest—one in Kosciusko, Mississippi, and the other in Brunswick, Georgia. All three were ladies who loved Jesus and poured out their lives in kindness to others. They are safely home with their Lord, and all is well. What about those of us who remain? How are we to go on?

A little book I gave my mom a few months after my dad's death in 1989 is titled *Jesus Wept* by Leroy Brownlow. This section that follows is instructive:

> The Lord is our Shepherd. The Shepherd has information not possessed by the sheep. Our knowledge is limited but the Shepherd knows beyond the hills there is a valley where life is pleasant.

The Shepherd has knowledge we don't have yet. He tells us all we need to know in His Holy Word. Let us go expectantly to our Bibles and read the following scriptures:

1 Corinthians 15:35–38
2 Corinthians 5:1–8
1 Thessalonians 4:13–18

If we obey, we will be comforted by these words, and then we who believe can reach out to others and comfort them with these same eternal promises. Good News? You better believe it!

The Song in the Storm

The other day I was outside while it was storming, and I heard the most incredible sound. Through the crashing thunder, flashing lightning, and splashing raindrops, I heard a bird singing its own sweet song—loudly, fearlessly, and joyfully! What an unlikely pair—the raging storm and the singing bird. As I rolled this wonder over in my mind, I began to think of other unlikely pairs.

The Labrador and orangutan pals recently featured on TV; my alter egos W. C. Monk, a stuffed ape and Rainbow the Clown; the lion and the lamb spoken of in scripture; the beauty and the beast in literature; my dog, Lady, and my outdoor cat, Surprise; and the deep friendships that develop between persons who greatly differ from one another in either age, race, beliefs, or nationality.

Most of all, I am in awe because of the most unlikely pair of all—God and I! Wow! No wonder that bird is always singing, even in the midst of a raging storm. It knows the Creator! Come to think of it, so do you and I. We know that God is not only our Creator but also our Redeemer. Listen! You can hear the bird singing loudly, fearlessly, and joyfully. Let's join in because we know the same song in our language: "Praise Him, praise Him, all ye little children. God is love, God is love." Once again now—loudly, fearlessly, and joyfully!

The Truth: Simple and Profound

Recently, I was looking through my collection of old LP records for a particular recording by Evie Tornquist Karlson, a Christian vocalist. When I found it, I played it for the first time in years. Hearing the featured selections again was just as inspiring as the first time I listened to it, which was some time in the late seventies or early eighties.

Right now I want you to join with me in this little faith exercise. Sing or recite to yourself the words from the song "Jesus Loves Me."

> Jesus loves me! This I know,
> For the Bible tells me so.
> Little ones to Him belong;
> They are weak, but He is strong.

Believe it! God's Word does not lie. Incorporated in Evie's vocal arrangement of "Jesus Loves Me" is an additional selection by Kurt Kaiser which is as follows:

> Oh, how He loves you and me.
> He gave His life, what more could He give;
> Oh, how He loves you, Oh, how He loves me,
> Oh, how He loves you and me.

Believe it! Rejoice! It's the best news you or anyone will ever hear! Why not tell someone today? Share the Good News. Tell someone about Jesus' love. God will honor your witness to His son.

The Unexpected Answer

Have you ever been speechless? I was recently at our family reunion. Let me set the scene for you. We had finished the formal program segment and had moved on to sampling the delicious foods everyone had brought. Some individuals were gathered in groups looking at pictures and newspaper clippings while others conversed in groups around the room.

One gentleman was sitting at a table by himself, and I went over to chat with him. Earlier in the day he had mentioned to the group that it was unusual for him to be present at a Sunday reunion as he pastored a church in the Calhoun City, Mississippi, area. He was dressed casually, had a good tan, seemed about average height, and was impressive in size. I walked over and said, "Hello, I'm Peggy Keady." We shook hands, and he introduced himself. I then said, "What size is your church?" He looked at me with puzzlement and did not respond, so I then said, "How big is your church?"

He finally blurted out, while fingering his shirt, "Well, I think this is a 4XL."

I was speechless and began to glow with the blush of embarrassment until I managed to utter, "No, *church*!" And then I spelled the word, "*C-H-U-R-C-H*!"

He replied, "Oh!" and his face widened into a relieved smile. I responded in like manner as he began to tell me not only the size of his church but a lot more.

He answered not only a question that I didn't ask, but one I would never ask! He heard me ask something I didn't ask, and his answer to the unasked question floored me. Later as my brother and I returned home, I found the exchange both humorous and thought provoking. I began to wonder both about the words I speak and about the words I hear. Have there been other times I have spoken and not been understood? Did I keep on until someone comprehended my message? How many times have I missed what someone was asking or telling me because I did not listen carefully? Wow! Talk about an encounter that makes one take stock. This was one for the books.

I thought about several scriptures that give guidance on this subject of listening and speaking such as the following:

> Everyone should be quick to listen, slow to speak and slow to become angry. (James 1:19 NIV)

> An anxious heart weighs a man down, but a kind word cheers him up. (Proverbs 12:25 NIV)

> A word aptly spoken is like apples of gold in settings of silver. (Proverbs 25:11 NIV)

I'll work on my enunciation and keep trying to communicate. How about you?

The View from Above

Recently, I was sitting in our Oxford cottage, looking out the glass doors and windows when I realized that the only thing I could see was green foliage! The cottage, situated on a hillside, is surrounded by trees with a beautiful lake down below. The cottage is an ideal place to relax and let your imagination take flight, so I did just that. I began to pretend that I was in a wonderful tree house high above the ground amid the trees' lush canopy. What a revealing mental adventure!

Allowing myself the freedom to pursue these mental images resulted in a different take on events, those occurring below me and those happening at a distance. I came to a new viewpoint. My way of looking at and interpreting life events was changed due to my elevated position and my God-created surroundings.

As I reviewed my choice to assume the "treetop mindset," I became aware that Christian thinking is just the same. We have a unique perspective on life. We live above the fray. We know the God who creates out of nothing and who brings beauty out of tragedy. We see with the eyes of faith. Every person is precious in God's sight, and He really does have the whole world in His hands. We see the world through His eyes. This renewing of our minds begins when we kneel at the cross and by grace become new creations. Then we think high thoughts and are surrounded and guided by the leaves of His Holy Word.

When you exit your prayer closet today, go look out your windows. I believe that you, like me, can have that "treetop mentality." After all, it's God's gift to us. Sometime today, read Romans 12:2 and 2 Corinthians 5:16–20 and give thanks. Viewing life from His tree house is awesome!

Time

"Tempus Fugit" Time Flies
"Tempus Neminem Manet" Time Waits for No One

Today is November 25, one month from Christmas Day. I can hardly catch my breath! It seems only a few days ago, we were all wondering when the terrific heat would let up. Now, here we are putting on fleece outfits to keep warm as winter's icy fingers come calling. Brrr!

All this brings to mind the truth that you and I are passing through time rapidly. Life here on earth is brief. Actually, the length of our individual lives is unknown to us, but not to God. Since He knows each of us so intimately, let's listen to His wisdom: "I tell you, now is the time of God's favor, now is the day of salvation" (2 Corinthians 6:2 NIV). This means we are to be about our Father's business, reading his Word, praying, giving thanks and praise, loving the people He sends into our lives, speaking a word of hope to the distressed, telling others the difference Jesus makes in our lives, and being willing to lead others to His cross and then on to the empty tomb. Alleluia!

O Lord, please help us to wisely use the time you have given us on earth. Amen.

Treasures

I am writing this on my sixty-ninth birthday having attended the homecoming at Sand Spring Presbyterian Church in Orwood, southwest of Oxford, Mississippi, where my brother, Bill, is a member. Our friends from Coffeeville, Mississippi, Alice and Jason Jordan, were in attendance as well. Family, faith, and friends are the recurring treasures in my life. I would suggest that this may be true for you, too, even though you may not have realized it.

It was in the family that I was born into where I came to faith. When I was a wee baby, my dear parents claimed the promises of God for my life through the sacred act of infant baptism and then walked before me as professing Christians. Many of their friends became my friends nurturing me through childhood and even into my young adult years.

My faith grew, and I professed Christ. I have attended many faith events in my life: World Mission Conferences at Montreat, North Carolina; several summers at Camp DeSoto in Mentone, Alabama; a Billy Graham Crusade at Madison Square Garden in New York; a summer session at the Presbyterian School of Christian Education in Richmond, Virginia; and several years of theological study at Biblical Seminary, now New York Theological Seminary, in New York, which involved field work in two churches and in one hospital in the metro area. In addition to being a church member wherever I lived and working on staff in four great churches, I came to know many wonderful individuals whose friendships blessed my life then and now as I recall with humble thanksgiving their sweet companionship. Each new adventure in my life is bounded on every side with fond memories of my grandmother, my parents, and my aunts and uncles, who now enjoy the perfect presence of the Lord Jesus Christ. I rejoice in the hours I spend with my brother and the times he and I visit with my nephew and his wife and son.

Take a few minutes now with a pencil in hand to check every

activity listed below that you have ever participated in or attended. Let's see if what I stated is true.

Faith
__ Bible study
__ Sunday school
__ Worship
__ Youth group
__ Summer camp
__ Church sports team
__ Camp/conference
__ Prayer group
__ Choir
__ Revival
__ Sacred music concert
__ Gospel singing
__ Passion play
__ Lay reader
__ Cursillo
__ Walk to Emmaus
__ Camp meeting
__ Visitation
__ Lay preaching
__ Helping hands
__ Charge conference
__ Vesper service
__ Hymn singing
__ Healing service
__ Prayer breakfast
__ Holiday happening
__ Bible Sunday

__ Christmas Eve service
__ Watch night vigil
__ Dinner on the grounds
__ Living nativity
__ Communion
__ Baptism
__ Helpline
__ Confirmation
__ Church committees
__ Circle meetings

Family
__ Reunions
__ Family traditions
__ Trips
__ Births
__ Weddings
__ Funerals

Friends
__ Elementary school
__ Junior High school
__ High school
__ College
__ Work
__ Church
__ Leisure time
__ Camp

If you have many checks, then you also have great treasures in the trinity of faith, family, and friends. Celebrate today! Let's say a prayer to our Creator, the God and Father of our Lord and Savior, Jesus Christ, for His immeasurable kindness to each one of us.

Trust

I once heard the statement, "In the midst of what you're planning and doing, life happens." How true! We can be going along with our daily routines—shopping, cooking, eating, working in the yard, attending sports events, keeping appointments, taking naps, watching TV, attending church—and whoosh, life happens!

One of these unexpected events breaks up our routine. The news can be really good or truly bad, but whatever it is, we are rocked internally and turned on our human axis to peer into a new depth we've never known. I am discovering that when "life breaks" in on me, now more than ever, I can trust the one who said:

> "Because he loves me," says the Lord, "I will rescue
> him; I will protect him, for he acknowledges my name.
> He will call upon me, and I will answer him; I will be
> with him in trouble, I will deliver him and honor him.
> With long life I will satisfy him and show him my
> salvation" (Psalm 91:14–16 NIV).

Turn and extend your hand, and His firm grasp will calm your mind and fill you with the most incredible joy-filled peace!

Unity

I have been rereading some of the materials that I have saved from past years and found one that I want to share with you since it is quite thought provoking. The article "Joined at the Head" by Paul Thigpen, was from issue 140 of the *Discipleship Journal*.

> What are the implications for the church of this living union with Jesus? (He is the Head and we are His Body.) First, if the Head and the Body are truly one, then we must never forget that however I treat the church, I treat Christ Himself. Do I nourish and care for the church, despite all its wounds and scars, or do I chronically complain about it? Am I loyal to it, or do I desert it as soon as the going gets rough? The Head and the Body are one. Which would I rather be: a pan of hot water for Christ's aching feet, or an annoying mosquito on His nail-scarred hand? ... In the life of the church, Jesus must come first, before anyone or anything else. Neither programs nor personalities nor petty politics can be allowed to take precedence over Him. When we get that priority straight, the rest falls into place. When we don't, the result is chaos.

Food for thought? You bet! Now let's revisit our Savior's words to His disciples:

> But you will receive power when the Holy Spirit comes on you; and you will be my witnesses in Jerusalem, and all Judea and Samaria, and to the ends of the earth (Acts 1:8 NIV).

Now I think I can see things clearly. How about you?

Voices

"Can you identify that voice? I would know it anywhere. It's ___ on the phone." Sound familiar? Well, I urge you to listen closely and to cherish hearing your loved one's unique voice because one day in the future you will long to hear it and not be able to for death will have silenced it.

I began to think about the numerous voices that have blessed me through the years; so many of them now silenced. What I would give to hear them again, and some day I will when God calls me home. Their voices encouraged, exhorted, cautioned, welcomed, inspired, praised, complimented, comforted, prepared, instructed, and caressed. All these voices have brought blessings to my life.

I want to be that voice for someone today. I will speak to others and honor the silence of the beloved voices from my past. I can choose each day to speak blessings into the lives of others. Scripture declares that the power of life and death is in the tongue (Proverbs 18:21). Here and now I choose life! You and I have the power to bless others with our words. I'm starting today! How about you?

Word Power

Do you like to work crossword puzzles? I do. My mother was a whiz, using a pen to complete them. I'm not there! I need an eraser and a good one at that. I was finishing a puzzle the other day and gave myself a "100" since I did not have to get any help from the answer page in the back of the book. I began to think about the word *crossword*.

The Bible declares that God created the world and all that is in it by speaking it into existence. The Bible also calls Jesus the "Logos, the Word made flesh," and the Bible is named the "Holy Word of God." We are told that words matter. We know that the old saying "Sticks and stones may break my bones, but words will never hurt me" is untrue. Words have power, great power! Words can either deliver hurt or deliver healing. No wonder we are instructed in James 3:1–18 to allow the Holy Spirit to take control of our tongues so that we may become messengers of healing rather than destruction.

Join me in completing a spiritual self-inventory if you will. Am I in my daily living, boastful, critical, bitter, selfish, or jealous, or am I becoming gentle, peace loving, courteous, open to discussion, willing to yield to others, full of mercy and good deeds, wholehearted, straightforward, and sincere? I can see from my self-inventory results that I have a way to go. Praise God, the Spirit is at work, and He says He will finish the work He has begun in both you and me. Today, let's thank Him for His wonderful transforming power at work in us for His glory!

Worthy Walks

The other night after hearing the sad news of Whitney Houston's death, I began to think of three exceptional black women, friends of mine, who touched my life in unique ways. They have completed their earthly walks and now stand in the presence of their Lord. As a preface to what I want to say, I draw to your attention that one of the current best-selling books and highly acclaimed films in the news is titled *The Help*. Then there is the popular daytime television show known as *The Talk*. Well, I choose to call this newsletter article "The Walk."

Enter lady 1: Delneather Chase.

Del, a widow in Greenville, Mississippi, was employed by my parents several days a week as a housekeeper and sometimes babysitter when my nephew was a child. She was a dear soul—so gentle, kind, and devoted to our family, to her duties, and to her God. Del often wrote to me little encouraging notes during the years I lived so far away in Georgia. When I would come, driving in for summer vacation or the Christmas holidays, her face would be wreathed in a smile as she exited the house with one or both of my parents. Her bearing was one of quiet dignity, and her work ethic was based on honesty and dependability.

While retired and in her eighties, she was murdered in her home in the fall of 1993. Upon receiving the shocking news and circumstances of her death, I was both crushed and filled with righteous indignation. How could anyone hurt such a sweet, precious lady?

Delneather Chase was like a gentle *giant walking* beside me.

Enter lady 2: Othareatha Mabry.

Mrs. Mabry became my friend as we worked together on staff for several years at Goodman-Pickens Elementary School in Goodman, Mississippi. She was a person of great zeal and good will. There was no subject which she and I could not discuss with each other. I felt her pain and joy, and she felt mine. In our conversations during break time, while on the job, we would move from the serious issues to the humorous ones with ease. After I retired, our mutual friendship continued with impromptu get-togethers and frequent phone chats. The news of her sudden death both stunned and saddened me.

Othareatha Mabry was like a *joyful light* walking beside me.

Enter lady 3: Shirley Frizell

At Goodman-Pickens Elementary School, Mrs. Frizell was the boss, and her leadership was excellent. I can testify to this because she was the fourteenth principal under whom I had worked. At the time I began work under her administration, I was in recovery from an unpleasant work experience. I found her way of doing things orderly, fair, and refreshing. The five years I had the privilege of working with her were not only very enjoyable but by far my most productive years as a school counselor. Mrs. Frizell gave her best and expected her staff to do the same. We often were able to meet her standard, and it felt good when we did. She was a woman of deep faith who displayed wisdom and love every day to each person who came her way. The news of her illness deeply grieved me, but I was blessed to have several sweet visits with her before she went to be with the Lord. Her death has left an empty place in my life.

Shirley Frizell was like a *ministering angel* walking beside me.

These three black women greatly inspired me and added a new dimension to my life by allowing me to walk beside them for a season. They walked with dignity, integrity, joy, and love. They didn't just talk these things; they walked them out every day. I salute them as successes in my world, and I give God the glory for their worthy walks. To my *gentle giant*, my *joyful light*, and my *ministering angel*, until we meet again, know that I will always love you.

The Invitation

O Come, All You Saints

Come as you are.
He will take your brokenness and make you whole.

Come as you are.
He will take your emptiness and fill you with peace.

Come as you are.
He will take your hurting and cover you with healing.

Come as you are.
He will take your doubts and flood you with hope.

Come as you are.
He will take your sadness and give you joy.

Come as you are.
He is waiting just for you to gather you in His everlasting arms.

You are His beloved.
Come, today, just as you are. Jesus, your Savior, is waiting!

About the Author

Peggy Keady is a retired educator and counselor who has worked in a variety of settings: public schools, churches, hospitals, and a nursing care facility.

Her extensive teaching and counseling experience give her writing a realistic flavor and a spiritual depth which readers will find both winsome and insightful.

Peggy holds degrees from the University of Mississippi, Oxford; New York Theological Seminary; Loyola University New Orleans; and Georgia Southern University, Statesboro, Georgia. Her areas of study were health, physical education and recreation, religious education, and counseling.

She has served in elementary, middle, and secondary public schools in Georgia, Louisiana, and Mississippi, first as a teacher and later as a counselor.

Peggy's pastoral care experiences include participation in chaplaincy training courses at Columbia-Presbyterian Medical Center, New York, and at Southern Baptist Hospital, New Orleans. Over the years, she worked on staff at the following churches: Madison Avenue Presbyterian Church, New York; First Presbyterian Church, New York; First Presbyterian Church, Brunswick, Georgia; St. Simons Presbyterian Church, St. Simons Island, Georgia; Rock Spring Presbyterian, Atlanta, Georgia; and First United Methodist, Kosciusko, Mississippi.

A native of Greenville, Mississippi, Peggy currently lives in Kosciusko, Mississippi, with her dog, Nick, her outside cat, Surprise, and her stuffed ape sidekick, W. C. Monk.

During her last five years as school counselor, she teamed up with W. C. Monk to give drug prevention programs and ballroom dance exhibitions. At church, Peggy and W. C. often presented children's sermons. In addition to W. C. Monk, her other alter ego, Rainbow the Clown, has entertained children of all ages.

References

Allen, Robert, and Al Stillman. "Moments to Remember." Song from the album *The Four Lads' Greatest Hits*. 1955.

Bart, Lionel. "Reviewing the Situation." Song in musical *Oliver!* 1963.

Brownlow, Leroy. *Jesus Wept: Trusting the Good Shepherd When You Lose a Loved One*. Forth Worth, TX: Brownlow Publishing, 1969.

Cahn, Sammy, and Jimmy Van Henson. "The Secret of Christmas." Song from film, "Say One for Me."1959.

Cahn, Sammy, and Jule Styne. "Let It Snow." Song from Dean Martin album, "A Winter Romance". Capitol (S) T-1285 Hollywood, CA: 1959.

Kaiser, Kurt. "Oh, How He Loves You and Me."Song. Evie Favorites, vol. 1. Waco, TX: Word, 1979.

Lynch, Sue. "Make New Friends." Accessed June 29, 2012. http://www.scoutsongs.com/lyrics/makenewfriends.html.

Moore, Clement Clarke. " A Visit from St. Nicolas " or "The Night Before Christmas." The Troy Sentinel, December 23, 1823.

Powell, Mac, and Third Day Band. " Born Again." Song . Evie Favorites, vol. 1, Waco, TX: Word, 1979.

"Praise Him, All You Little Children." Anon.
Music by Carey Bonner, (1859-1938).

Rankin, Jeremiah E. "God Be With You". *The Cokesbury Worship Hymnal. Nashville,TN: Abingdon Press, 1966*.

Rossi, Melody. *May I Walk You Home? Sharing Christ's Love with the Dying*. Bloomington, MN: Bethany House, 2007.

Thigpen, Paul. "Joined at the Head." *Discipleship Journal,* #140 (2004): 44. Used by Permission of Discipleship Journal. Copyright © 2004. The Navigators. Used by permission of NavPress. All rights reserved.

Warner, Anna B. "Jesus Loves Me." Song. *Evie Favorites*, vol. 1, Waco, TX: Word Music, 1979.

Printed in the United States
By Bookmasters